LIVING THINGS

ROBERT SNEDDEN

Fungus

FRANKLIN WATTS
LONDON • SYDNEY

Designed by Guy Callaby
Edited by Pip Morgan
Illustrations by Guy Callaby
Picture research by Su Alexander

ISBN 978 07496 7554 7

Dewey Classification: 579.6

A CIP catalogue for this book is available from the British Library.

Picture acknowledgements

Title page Scott T. Smith/Corbis; 3 Michael Maconachie;
Papilio/Corbis; 4 Dennis Johnson;
Papilio/Corbis; 5t Bengt Lundberg/Nature Picture Library, b Steve Axford; 7 Visuals
Unlimited/Corbis; 8 Nick Garbutt/Nature Picture Library; 9t Visuals Unlimited/Corbis,
b George McCarthy/Nature Picture Library; 10 Robert Pickett/Corbis; 11 Clouds Hill
Imaging Ltd/Corbis; 12 Philippe Clement/Nature Picture Library; 13t Micro Discovery/
Corbis, b Michael Maconachie; Papilio/Corbis; 14 Bernard Castelein/Nature Picture Library;
15t Vaughan Fleming/Science Photo Library, b Kevin Thiele; 16 Scott T. Smith/Corbis;
17 John Howard/Science Photo Library; 18 Niall Benvie/Corbis; 19t Geoff Simpson/Nature
Picture Library, b Raymond Gehman/Corbis; 21t Hal Horwitz/Corbis, b Dr Jeremy Burgess/
Science Photo Library; 22 Brian Hawkes/NHPA; 23t Asgeir Helgestad/Nature Picture Library,
b Solvin Zankl/Nature Picture Library; 24 Patrick Johns/Corbis; 25 Visuals Unlimited/Corbis;
26 Bob Sacha/Corbis; 27t Becky Luigart-Stayner/Corbis, b Lester V. Bergman/Corbis; 28 Ray
and Elma Kearney; 29t ParkNet/NPS.Gov, b Fred Stevens.

Front cover: Pat O'Hara/Corbis

Printed in China

Contents

What is a fungus?

People sometimes think of fungi (the plural of fungus) as types of plant, but they're not. They stay in one place as plants do, but they aren't green and can't make their own food using sunlight.

Although they get their food by consuming other living (or once living) things as animals do, they aren't animals. In fact, fungi are very different from both plants and animals and have their own special place in the living world – the fungi kingdom.

Fungi and you

You've almost certainly come across fungi in many forms. Mushrooms are the most familiar types of fungus. You may very well have eaten some on your pizza. You might have seen fungi sprouting up in a woodland or growing on a dead tree trunk.

BELOW *Mica cap mushrooms grow on dead wood all over North America. When they are young they glisten in the light.*

Some members of the fungus kingdom may not be so familiar or so obvious. If you've ever thrown away food which has gone bad or a piece of mouldy bread, you've thrown out a fungal colony with it because the moulds are fungi, too. The yeast that made the bread rise when it was made is also a fungus. And if you've ever suffered from itchy feet caused by athlete's foot you have a fungus to thank for that as well.

Digging deeper

There is usually more to a fungus than what you see. A mushroom, for example, is just one part of a fungus. A mushroom's relationship to the whole fungus is similar to an apple's relationship to an apple tree. In this book we'll dig a little deeper into the world of the fungi and learn what makes them different from other living things, and how they fit into the natural world in some very important ways.

ABOVE *Morels, like these ones growing in Sweden, are a tasty edible fungus and are prized for cooking.*

WOW!

The world's biggest known fungus was found in a forest in Michigan in the US. It extends through 150,000 square metres of soil and is thought to weigh over 10,000 kilograms – that's more than two good-sized elephants!

LEFT *Blue pixie's parasol mushrooms grow on both sides of the Pacific Ocean – in Australia, New Zealand and Chile.*

Chains of cells

For a long time scientists put plants and fungi together. Then when the microscope was invented, many of the differences between plants and fungi became clear.

Scientists used to class fungi as plants because the most obvious examples of fungi – mushrooms – grow in soil, just as plants do. They certainly look more like funny little plants than animals. But not all fungi are mushrooms, and they don't all grow in the soil.

The world of the cell

The smallest part of a living thing is called a cell. Some of your cells are blood cells, some are nerve cells, some form your skin and others form your heart, kidneys, lungs and other parts of your body. Plants also have different kinds of cell that make up their leaves, stems and roots. Fungi are different, because their cells are all the same.

The cells of both plants and fungi are surrounded by a rigid cell wall. But plant cell walls are made of cellulose, whereas fungal cell walls are made of chitin. This is the same substance that forms the tough outer skeletons of insects and spiders.

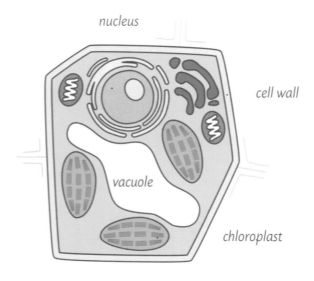

nucleus

cell wall

vacuole

chloroplast

LEAF CELL
Each leaf cell has a nucleus that controls what happens within it. Chloroplasts make food from sunlight and a vacuole can fill with water and substances such as sugar.

A network of chains

The cells of a fungus form long, very thin chains. These threads of fungus cells are called hyphae (pronounced hi-fee). One thread is called a hypha (hi-fer). Together, a branching network of hyphae forms a mycelium (my-see-li-um), which is the body of the fungus. The hyphae form a complex system of microscopic tubes. Nutrients flow through this from one part of the mycelium to another.

If you look under leaf litter in a woodland you might find some cobwebby strands of hyphae in the soil. These keep on growing as long as they have enough food and moisture to keep them alive. They can grow longer, but never wider, though a number of hyphae may grow alongside each other, like threads forming a rope. When conditions are right the hyphae produce mushrooms.

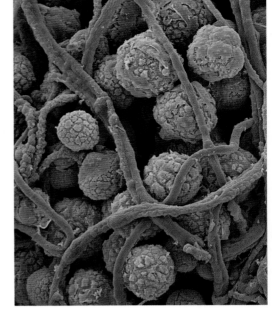

ABOVE *This is a highly magnified photograph of a mould called* Epicoccum purpurascens, *which is common in the air and soil. It can cause spots to form on the leaves of plants. The red spheres are its spores and the brown strands are hyphae.*

One-cell fungi

Not all fungi form chains of hyphae. Some, such as yeasts, live as single cells and form colonies with millions and millions of individuals. There are several types of yeast. Some, such as the type we use to make bread, are useful. Others can give us nasty infections.

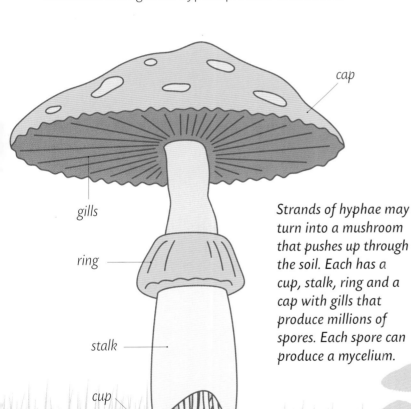

cap

gills

ring

stalk

cup

hypha

Strands of hyphae may turn into a mushroom that pushes up through the soil. Each has a cup, stalk, ring and a cap with gills that produce millions of spores. Each spore can produce a mycelium.

7

Mushrooms and more

If a fungus is made up of a network of microscopically fine hyphae where do mushrooms fit into the picture? The answer is that they are also formed from hyphae.

Fruits of the fungi

Just as flowering plants have flowers and fruits, so many fungi produce mushrooms. Both have the same job to do – to ensure that there will be another generation of plants, or in this case, fungi. In the same way that a fruit tree grows all year round but only produces fruits at a certain time of year, so the mycelium only produces mushrooms when conditions are right. Just as a fruit has seeds inside that can grow into new plants, so a mushroom produces microscopically small spores, which are the fungus equivalent of seeds.

Fruiting bodies

Mushrooms are also called fruiting bodies. Different types of fungus have different fruiting bodies that are formed from closely-packed hyphae strands. As well as the familiar mushrooms with their stalks and caps, there are many others, including bracket fungi, which look a bit like dinner plates embedded in the sides of trees, and the spherical puffballs.

RIGHT *These bracket fungi growing on a tree in Madagascar may look attractive, but the threads of hyphae growing inside the tree will eventually kill it.*

Budding

Single-celled yeasts don't produce fruiting bodies. Once a yeast cell reaches a certain size a small growth, or bud, begins to appear. The bud grows bigger and bigger until eventually it breaks away to become a new yeast cell in its own right. This is called budding.

RIGHT *The buds on these yeast cells will eventually break away to form new yeast cells.*

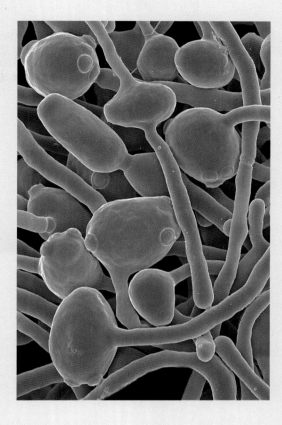

Fairy rings

A mycelium growing through the ground forms an expanding ring, rather than a disc. This happens because the central part of the mycelium dies as the hyphae use up the food available. The fungus finds new food sources only at the outer part of the mycelium. The mushrooms that grow in this 'fairy ring' mark the outer part of the circular mycelium hidden beneath the ground.

LEFT *This fairy ring of mushrooms marks the outer edge of a fungus.*

Spores, spores, spores

Fungi produce spores – millions and millions of them. A single giant puffball can release over 0 million million spores, each one of which might become a new puffball mycelium.

Gill and chain

If you look at the underside of a mushroom cap you will see that it has a number of fine sheets. These are called gills and it is here that the spores form. Mould fungi, the type you see growing on old pieces of bread, don't produce mushrooms. Instead, vertical hyphae grow up from the mycelium. These hyphae have a powdery appearance because they are covered in millions of spores that grow in chains along the hyphae. Depending on the type of mould they might be blue-green, brown-black or reddish pink in colour.

WOW!

Stinkhorns are a type of fungus that attract flies to help spread their spores. They live up to their name as some smell like rotting meat and others like fresh dog faeces.

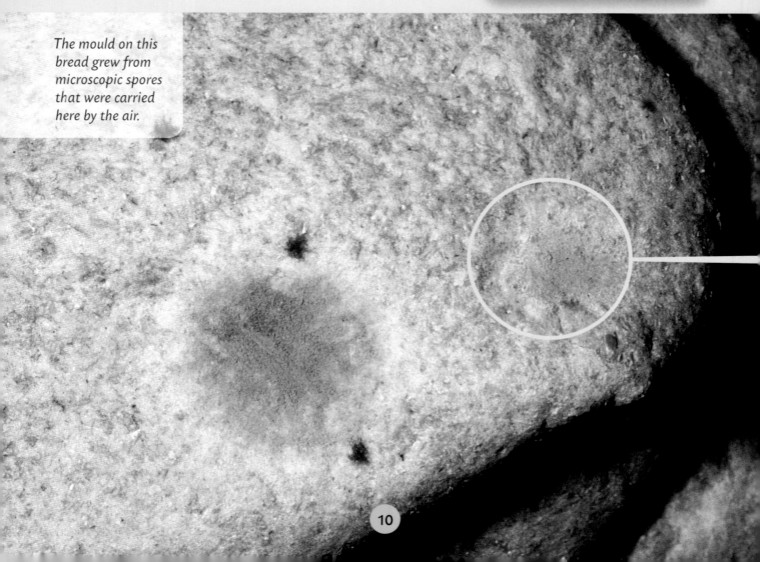

The mould on this bread grew from microscopic spores that were carried here by the air.

Spore prints

Mushrooms that look similar can sometimes be told apart by the colour of their spores. Making a spore print is easy. Just cut the stem off a mushroom (freshly picked – not from the supermarket) and lay the cap half on white paper and half on black. (The black paper will show you if the mushroom has white spores.) Cover with a bowl and leave for several hours. Remove the bowl and very carefully pick up the cap. Underneath there should be a pattern of spores that matches the gill pattern of the mushroom.

Air spores

Fungus spores are so tiny and light that they can be carried for great distances on air currents. There are so many spores around that you probably take in a few every time you draw a breath. Because they are so small spores, unlike seeds, do not carry a store of food. If they land by a suitable food source they will begin to grow almost at once.

Before very long, if the conditions are right, each new mycelium will produce its own spores. With these countless millions of spores floating through the air ready to colonize fresh food sources it is hardly any wonder that our food goes bad so quickly!

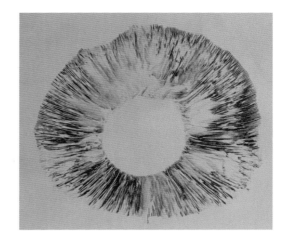

ABOVE *This gill pattern is formed from millions of spores from the underside of a mushroom cap.*

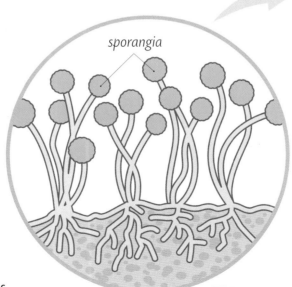

sporangia

spore germinates

FUNGUS SPORES

The mycelium of the bread mould produces spore sacs (sporangia) on the top of stalks. When a sac breaks open, thousands of spores are released into the air. If they find somewhere suitable to grow they germinate and start a new mcycelium.

11

A tour of the kingdom

The fungus kingdom can be roughly divided into three groups: club fungi, sac fungi and zygomycetes (pronounced zi-go-my-seats). Each is distinguished by the way they produce spores.

Club fungi

The fruiting bodies of club fungi are what most of us have in mind when we think of fungi. This group contains the most familiar mushrooms. There are around 25,000 club fungi, such as chanterelles, stinkhorns, puffballs and the common field mushrooms you find in the supermarket. It also includes plant pests such as smuts and rusts.

Club fungi bear their spores on microsopic club-shaped structures. They may form at the end of tiny threads in rusts and smuts, or on the exposed surface of the gills of mushrooms. Puffballs hide their spores inside and release them when the mushroom is broken.

LEFT *The shaggy inkcap is a typical club fungus. As it gets older its cap starts to dissolve into a black inky liquid.*

WOW!

Scientists have found a fungus that uses a noose formed by a hypha to catch tiny worms in the soil. Other hyphae grow into a captured worm and digest it.

Sac fungi

There are more than 30,000 different kinds of sac fungi. They form spores inside little sac-shaped structures. These may look like shallow cups, flasks or globes in shape, and are held within tightly-woven strands of hyphae.

Sac fungi contain all sorts of fungi. These include edible morel and truffle mushrooms, very useful yeasts and fungi that give flavour to cheeses such as Camembert and Stilton.

Zygomycetes

This is the branch of the fungi kingdom that includes bread moulds. Spore sacs grow on the top of stalked hyphae that emerge from the mycelium. They may also form spore-containing structures called zygospores. These can remain dormant for many months if they don't have the right conditions for growth.

Other fungi

Finally, there are some left-over fungi that are tricky to place in any group. They are called imperfect because no one has discovered what sort of spores they produce. The fungus that causes athlete's foot is one of these imperfect fungi.

ABOVE *Bread moulds are zygomycete fungi. Bunches of spore sacs form at the end of hyphae. This photograph is magnified 75 times.*

RIGHT *The scarlet elf cup is a sac fungus that produces spores on the inner surface of the cup.*

13

Fungus food

One obvious difference between fungi and plants is that fungi aren't green. This is because they don't have the chemical called chlorophyll, which plants use to trap the sun's energy to make sugars.

Most fungi feed on the dead remains of plants and animals, or their wastes. These fungi do a valuable job of recycling nutrients in the living world. They grow in woodlands where there is a lot of dead plant material for them to feed on. You will often see fungi growing on fallen branches, for example.

The honey fungus feeds on dead and decaying roots and tree stumps. It can also infect and eventually kill healthy plants.

Living on others

Some fungi are parasites, which means they take their nutrients from living animals and plants, and so harm the organism they feed from. Parasitic fungi can do a lot of damage to living trees. You see large bracket fungi jutting out like shelves from the side of a tree. This is a sign that hyphae threads are spreading through the tree, consuming it from within. The bracket fungus will eventually weaken and kill the tree, leaving a hollow trunk behind.

Eating with enzymes

Fungi have to break down, or digest, material produced by other living things to get the nutrients they need. Animals eat their food and break it down inside their bodies to absorb the nutrients. Fungi, on the other hand, break down their food before they absorb it.

Your digestive system produces chemicals called enzymes that break down the food you eat so that your body can use it. Fungi produce enzymes, too, but they come out of the fungus and on to the surface of whatever the fungus is feeding on. Fungi that attack plants produce enzymes that break down plant cell walls, but which have no effect on the chitin walls that protect the fungal cells. The enzymes dissolve the fungus's food, making it into a nutritious 'soup' that the fungus can absorb.

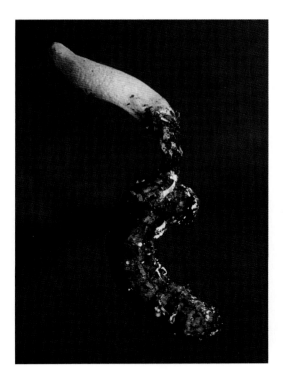

ABOVE *This caterpillar has been infected and killed by a parasitic fungus.*

WOW!

Fungi eat slowly – it can take a hundred years for the fungi living on the trunk of a hardwood tree to consume it.

LEFT *This Australian cup fungus lives on rotting wood in damp places.*

Clean-up squad

Most fungi feed on the remains of dead plants and animals. Along with bacteria, fungi are the most important part of the natural world's clean-up and recycling squad.

ABOVE *Layers of turkey-tail fungus growing on a log are a good sign that a lot of decomposing is going on!*

Decomposers

Fungi are important to the well-being of plants as they ensure that the nutrients in dead leaves and other remains are quickly and efficiently recycled. When a fungus breaks down, or decomposes, its meal it does not absorb all the 'soup' that it makes. Much of it leaks away into the ground to provide a vital source of nutrition for the plants growing nearby.

Soil conditioning

Many fungi help to maintain the health of the soil in other ways. The hyphae produce sticky substances that bind the tiny particles in the soil together. This creates spaces in the soil that allows air and water to filter through more easily so that plant roots can reach them.

Destruction

Fungi do their job of decomposing so well that often they attack things that we'd rather they left alone. Dry rot is a type of fungus that can damage buildings. Timbers affected by dry rot can become brittle and crumble into powder. This is something we'd want to avoid in our homes, but in the natural world it is an essential process.

Fungi quickly infect dead and dying trees and begin the process of breaking them down. If there were no fungi to break down the tree it would just stay there. New trees would have no room to grow, and no minerals in the soil to use. The dry rot fungus cannot tell the difference between a dead tree in the forest and the wood we take from that tree to use in our buildings.

LEFT *Dry rot can seriously damage a house, but the fungus does an important recycling job in woodland.*

Lichens

Fungi can form close relationships with other living things, particularly plants. Sometimes these can be harmful, as when plants are destroyed by fungal parasites. But some partnerships between plant and fungi can benefit both.

Lichens (pronounced lie-kens) are beneficial partnerships between fungi and microscopic algae (al-gee), which are a sort of plant. The two work so closely together that they could be thought of as a single living thing. Together, a fungus and an alga form a tough organism that can live in places where other living things would struggle to survive.

WOW!

The first person to realize that lichens were two different living things working together was children's author Beatrix Potter, famous for her books about Mrs Tiggywinkle and Peter Rabbit.

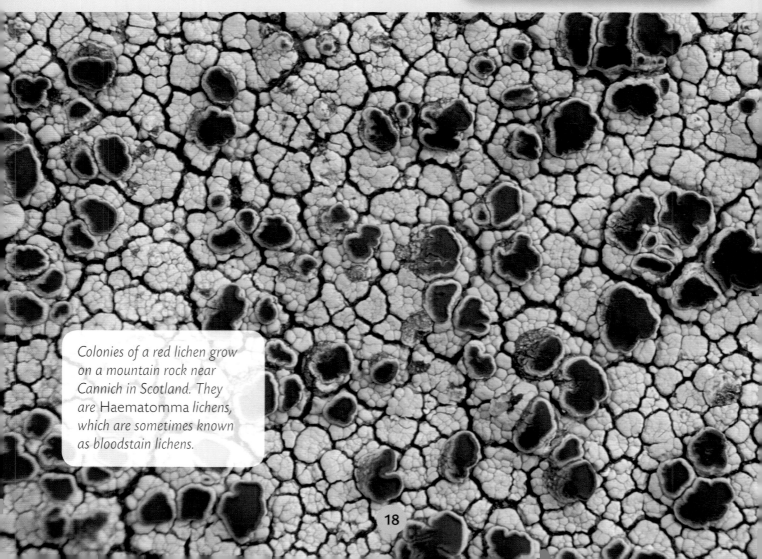

Colonies of a red lichen grow on a mountain rock near Cannich in Scotland. They are Haematomma *lichens, which are sometimes known as bloodstain lichens.*

Teamwork

Lichens live everywhere, from the bitter cold of the poles to the warmth of the tropical forests. They grow on gateposts and walls, on the bark of trees and on windswept mountaintops. They can colonize places where there are no other living things, growing on bare rock surfaces and cooled lava from volcanoes.

Lichens succeed by teamwork. The algae, like larger plants, make sugars using sunlight energy and provide the lichen with a source of food. At the same time, the fungus helps to prevent the alga from drying out in an exposed position, such as a rock surface. The fungus also produces chemicals that start to break down the surface of the rock, releasing valuable minerals that both need to grow.

Types of lichen

Lichens come in a variety of forms. Some are flat, growing close to the surface they cling to and forming a crust over the rock. Others are leaf-like and upright. The fungus almost always makes up the largest part of the lichen.

Clean air monitors

Lichens are sensitive to pollution in the air. Car exhaust emissions and fumes from factories can kill lichens. If you are lucky enough to live where there are lots of lichens it means that the air around you is fairly clean.

ABOVE *Some people in British Columbia, Canada, use this sunburst lichen to make a colour for their face paints.*

WOW!

A lichen may take a thousand years to grow just five centimetres.

LEFT *An old man's beard lichen hangs from the branches of trees. It grows in damp forests all over the world.*

Fungus roots

One of the most important relationships between fungi and plants takes place under the ground. Here, plant roots and fungi twine together to form a partnership that many plants couldn't live without.

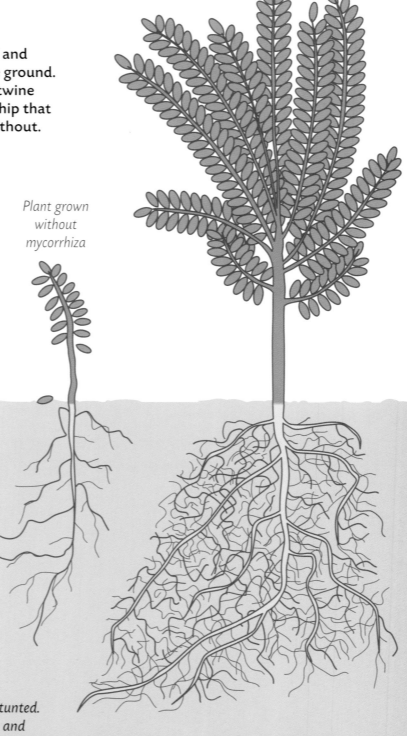

Plant grown without mycorrhiza

Plant grown with mycorrhiza

Working together

The alliance between plant roots and fungi is called a mycorrhiza (pronounced my-cor-ry-za), which means 'fungus root'. Fungus roots grow mostly in young trees, particularly in pine, birch and beech forests. About four-fifths of all plants have some fungus roots.

Plants do not grow as well without their fungus partners. The fungus spreads out through the soil, absorbing minerals and passing some of them on to the plant roots. The fungus increases the area of soil that the plant roots can reach on their own by between 100 and 1000 times. In turn, the fungus takes sugars from the plant roots.

Some fungi cover the plant roots completely. Others penetrate the roots and grow inside them, as well as spreading out into the soil.

HELPING PLANTS GROW

A plant without its fungus partner is small and stunted. A plant with mycorrhiza has a broad root system and grows taller, with more leaves. A healthy plant produces more food for the fungus, too!

Orchids and fungi

Some orchids depend on fungi to live. Orchid seeds are tiny and carry little food for the growing seedling. They will not germinate unless a fungus infects them. The orchid relies on the fungus for all its food needs until it has grown past the seedling stage. Some orchids are never able to make their own food and depend on the fungus all their lives.

One type of orchid shares its fungus partner with a tree. The fungus takes sugars from the tree roots and passes them on to the orchid!

WOW!

If you could take all the fungal hyphae growing around the roots of just one tree and stretch them out into a straight line it would be long enough to go several times around the world.

RIGHT *The striped coral root orchid cannot make its own food like other plants. It depends on its mycorrhizal fungi for nutrients.*

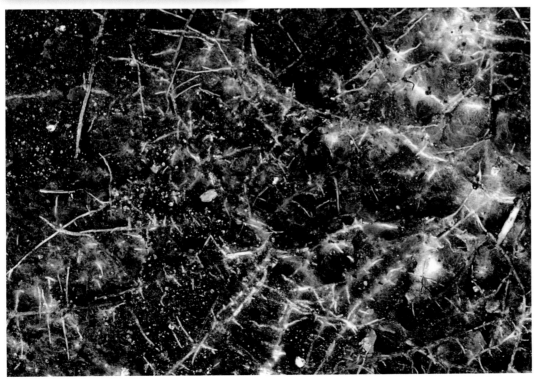

LEFT *The hyphae of this mycorrhizal fungus closely cover the roots of its plant partner.*

Fungus feeders

Anything that was once alive can be broken down to provide food for some fungus or other. But what about things that are still alive, and enjoy a tasty fungus snack?

A warning

There are fungi that taste very good, such as ceps, chanterelles and field mushrooms. But some mushrooms can make you very ill indeed, and some may even kill you if you eat them. It is very easy to confuse a harmless mushroom with a deadly one. So do not pick and eat mushrooms unless you are with an experienced guide.

LEFT *The name of the destroying angel is well deserved. It looks a little like an edible mushroom but it is deadly poisonous.*

Deer and squirrels also eat fungi. In cold northern regions reindeer depend on lichens for food. Often, particularly in winter, lichens are all the reindeer have to eat. They may even have to dig down into the snow to find them.

Fungi farmers

Some termites, ants and beetles grow fungi for food. Leafcutter ants, for example, don't eat the leaves that they snip from plants. They chew the leaves into a pulp, which they store in their nests. A fungus grows on the leaf pulp, and this is what the ants eat. It is their only source of food. Ambrosia beetles grow fungi along the walls of their burrows. They damage trees by burrowing into them and infecting them with fungi.

Not all fungi produce spores above ground where they can be spread around by the wind. Some fungi fruit underground. These fungi, such as truffles, rely on foraging animals to dig up their fruiting bodies. Some of the spores pass through an animal's body unharmed when the animal eats the fungus. They will be deposited elsewhere, complete with a package of animal droppings to grow in.

ABOVE *During the winter reindeer depend on lichens growing on rocks beneath the snow.*

Fungi food chains

We have already seen the part fungi play at the end of the food chain as decomposers and recyclers. They can also be important links higher up the food chain. Many types of insect, such as mites, fruit flies and gnats, and other tiny soil organisms feed on fungi.

RIGHT *A leafcutter ant carries a piece of leaf to its nest where it will be used to feed the colony's fungus garden.*

Fungi foes

Many fungi damage other living things. Fungi can be serious crop pests and they can also cause disease in humans and other animals.

Destructive diseases

Fungus diseases probably destroy about a tenth of the world's food crops. Invading fungi can damage cereal crops, such as wheat and corn, and fruit trees, such as pears and apples. A fungus that was spread from tree to tree by bark beetles killed millions of elm trees across Europe and North America in the 20th century.

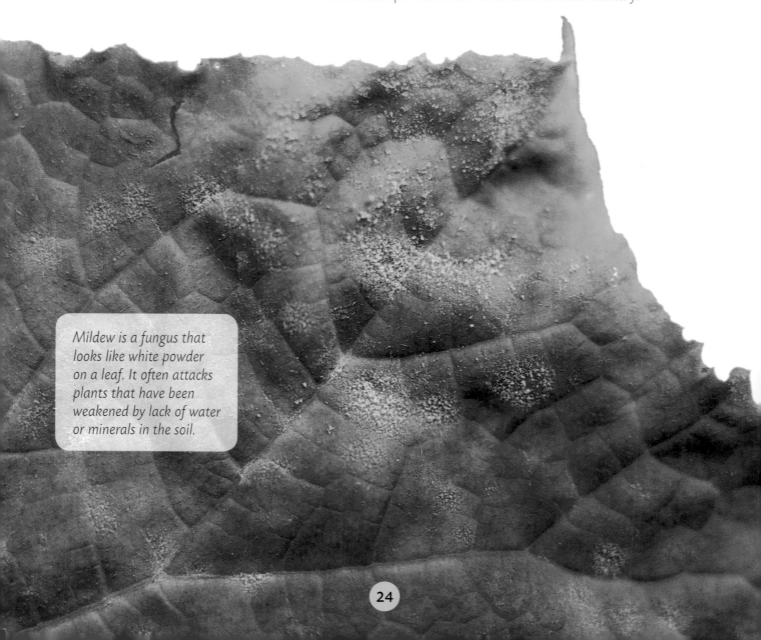

Mildew is a fungus that looks like white powder on a leaf. It often attacks plants that have been weakened by lack of water or minerals in the soil.

Some fungi attack the roots of a plant, while others attack the leaves. Mildews, for example, grow on leaves, making them look as if they are covered by a fine white powder. Rusts are a serious pest of fruits and cereals. They form dark, reddish, rust-like patches of spores on the infected plant. These fungi can cause leaves to fall and prevent buds from developing properly.

Fungus on us

Fungi will grow anywhere moist enough where there is something for them to feed on – and that includes parts of the human body. There are three ways fungi can harm humans. Some people have an allergic reaction to fungi and their spores; some fungi produce poisons, called mycotoxins; and others can actually grow in or on the body.

Some fungi grow in the outer layers of the skin. Athlete's foot is one of the most common of these fungal skin infections. This can be very annoying but it is not life-threatening, though there are some fungi that are. Cryptococcus, for example, is a type of fungus that can infect the membrane that surrounds the brain and cause the serious illness meningitis. Other fungi can form colonies in the lungs, causing dangerous infections.

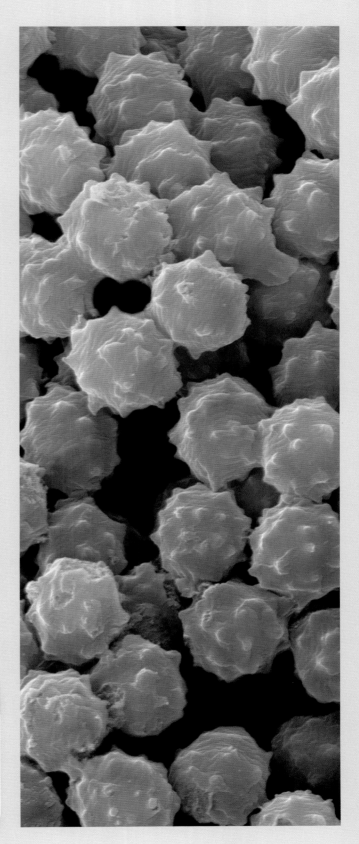

RIGHT *Colonies of this fungus, called* Aspergillus fumigatus, *often live in our pillows.*

WOW!

There might be as many as 16 different kinds of microscopic fungi living in your pillow. They feed on dead human skin and the droppings of dust mites.

Fungi friends

Over the centuries humans have found many uses for fungi besides simply eating some of them. Fungi play a vital role in very different processes, from producing fizzy drinks to ensuring the safe recovery of transplant patients.

Aspergillus niger *is a common household mould used to produce citric acid for soft drinks.*

Fungus cola

Fungi are used in the preparation of foods, such as soy sauce. Citric acid, found in many soft drinks and foods, was originally extracted from citrus fruits, such as limes and lemons. In 1917, a way was found to make it more cheaply by using fungi and now almost all the citric acid in soft drinks is made this way.

Yeasts

Perhaps the most widely used fungi are yeasts. Yeasts live in soil and on fruits and leaves. They play an important part in decomposition. Since ancient times bakers have used yeasts to make dough rise. As a yeast multiplies and grows inside the dough it produces bubbles of carbon dioxide gas, which makes the bread rise.

Other yeasts are used to produce alcoholic drinks. In a process called fermentation, yeast converts sugars from wheat, barley, rice and corn into carbon dioxide and alcohol. When grapes are crushed during wine making, the yeasts that grow on the grapeskins come into contact with sugars inside the grapes.

ABOVE *Yeasts allow us to make and enjoy a wide variety of different types of bread.*

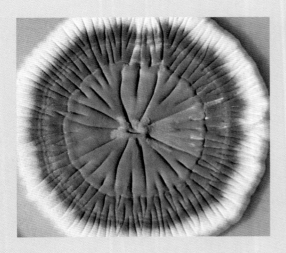

ABOVE *This is a colony of penicillium mould. Scientists made the first antibiotic, called penicillin, from this type of mould.*

Medical fungi

A mould similar to the one that grows on stale bread can kill many disease-causing bacteria. The mould produces penicillin, which was the first antibiotic to be discovered. Many antibiotics in daily use were first found in fungi. Fungi produce these antibiotics naturally to defend themselves.

A drug called cyclosporin, which is used to treat patients who have had organ transplants, also comes from a fungus. This drug helps the body to accept the new heart, kidney or other donated organ.

WOW!

Every year people eat eight million tonnes of mushrooms. More than half the world's mushrooms grown for eating come from China.

Fungus among us

There are fungi everywhere. No one is quite sure just how many different kinds there are. Around a hundred thousand different fungi, including mushrooms, moulds and mildews of various types, have been identified so far. The numbers of fungi waiting to be discovered and named may stretch to over a million.

Hidden kingdom

Fungi are one of the less obvious parts of the natural world. The mycelium and its network of hyphae are usually hidden from our sight, spreading through the soil, or through dead wood, endlessly probing for new food sources. We usually only notice them when they produce mushrooms, and only about a tenth of the fungi we know about have mushrooms or similar fruiting bodies.

BELOW *This is one of the world's rarest fungi. It is called* Hygrocybe callucera *and it lives in a small area near Sydney, Australia.*

No fungi, no forests?

Many fungi are sensitive to pollution. Fungi in forests seem to be disappearing at a disturbing rate, both in numbers and in variety. Tree roots and fungi have an vital partnership, so when fungi disappear trees lose an important part of their life-support system. Trees become more vulnerable to changes in their environment, such as water shortages. Logging certainly threatens the forests, but the disappearance of mushrooms may do so, too.

Although some fungi are harmful, most get the nutrients they need from dead material. Without them, and bacteria, the rest of the living world would have been buried long ago beneath its rubbish and remains.

We all benefit from the existence of fungi. If fungi did not act as recyclers, plants would not have the nutrients they need to grow. Without plants, we would all starve. Without fungi life could not go on as it does.

RIGHT *The blue bolbitius is a rare fungus that lives in Virginia, USA.*

WOW!

Fungi make up 90 per cent of the weight of living things in the soil of a typical forest, not counting the tree roots. The weight of fungi in the soil of a 100-metre square field is equivalent to 25 sheep walking on it.

LEFT *These fungi are called acrobatic earthstars. They look like tiny human figures. The 'head' of the fungus is its spore case.*

Glossary

Algae (singular alga)   Simple plants that usually live in or near water. They range from seaweeds to single-celled organisms.

Antibiotics   Chemicals taken from moulds and bacteria and used to treat infectious diseases.

Budding   A simple way for an organism such as yeast to reproduce itself; a new yeast cell develops by growing out of an existing cell.

Cell   The smallest unit of a living thing; some organisms are made up of a single cell, while larger organisms such as humans have trillions of cells.

Cellulose   A strong substance in the walls of plant cells.

Chitin   A strong substance in the cell walls of fungi and in the outer coverings of insects, crabs, spiders and other animals.

Chlorophyll   A chemical that captures sunlight energy for use in photosynthesis; it gives plants their green colour.

Decomposition   The process of decay; plant and animal remains break down into simpler parts that living things can reuse.

Enzymes   Substances in living things that can speed up a chemical process, such as the breakdown of food.

Faeces (pronounced fee-sees) The waste material produced and excreted from an animal's digestive system.

Fermentation   A natural process in which sugars are turned into alcohol.

Fruiting body   The part of a fungus that contains its spores; a mushroom is the fruiting body of a fungus.

Germinate   To begin to grow; a spore germinates into a new fungus.

Gills   Thin sheets where spores are formed under the caps of mushrooms.

Hyphae   Threadlike chains of fungus cells.

Mildew   A type of fungus that grows on living plants; the mycelium and spores of mildew form a powdery white growth on the plant's leaves.

Minerals   Simple chemicals that living things need to stay healthy; fungi get their minerals from their food.

Mould   A type of fungus that forms a furry growth on the surface of food and other materials; often found in damp places.

Mycelium   The network of hyphae that form the 'body' of a fungus.

Mycorrhiza   The partnership of a plant root system and a fungus mycelium; when they grow together the mycorrhiza brings benefits to both. Also called fungus roots.

Mycotoxins   Poisons that some fungi produce.

Nutrients   Substances that are essential for healthy life and growth.

Parasite   An organism that lives in or on another living thing, taking nourishment and causing harm.

Rust   A type of fungus that causes disease in plants. Rusts can often be seen as orange-red patches on the leaves.

Smut   A type of fungus that causes disease in plants. Smuts have masses of powdery, dark and sometime smelly spores.

Spore   The seed of a fungus that grows into a new mycelium if conditions are right.

Websites

http://www.virtualmuseum.ca/~mushroom/ English/
The Fungus Among Us: a fun introduction to the world of fungi from the Nova Scotia Museum of Natural History.

http://tomvolkfungi.net/
Fungi enthusiast Professor Tom Volk of the University of Wisconsin shares his knowledge.

http://herbarium.usu.edu/fungi/FunFacts/ factindx1.htm
Some fun facts about fungi.

http://www.nhm.ac.uk/nature-online/life/ plants-fungi/webcast-fantasticfungivid/ fantastic-fungi.html
Chef Antonio Carluccio talks about how fantastic fungi are – especially to eat!

Index